The Little Book of Swimming Safely

Sue Gyford

To Mum and Dad,
with thanks for dunking me in the sea early.

With thanks to The Wild Ones,
especially the first few.

In fond memory of Jim,
the Wild Ones' very own mermaid.

Introduction

This book arose out of the joy and hysteria of being an admin on two wild swimming facebook groups, during what I'll lovingly call The Great Influx of 2020.

Lockdown, cabin fever, the closure of swimming pools, a craving for novelty, and the inability to fly to Magaluf, all contributed to a huge increase in the number of people heading to beaches, rivers and lochs near home to swim.

After a brief period when wild swim admins around the country considered burning facebook down and diving into the waves forever, we calmed down and realised that we could hardly stop all these new folk from taking part in the activity that we loved so dearly, and nor should we, so we'd better get on with helping them do it safely.

It was a big ask – we could no longer swim in groups, so at the very moment the hordes headed for the water, we lost the ability to lead by example or pass on scraps of advice over our shivery bites.

As the weather got colder, our introductory posts for new members became ever more baroque, supplemented by guides to warming up and bans on boasting about how long you'd stayed in the water.

Amid all this cheerful chaos, one day, while adding 60 new members who'd asked in the space of a single week to join our group for a tiny pocket-sized beach, I thought "Well, this introductory post has got so long, it's practically a book." Then I realised that was not such a bad idea.

And so, welcome to The Little Book of Swimming Safely. The advice offered is particularly important for swimming in winter, but most of it is useful year-round. And while it talks a lot about the sea, because that's where I swim most, much of it is applicable to fresh water too.

It is by no means complete, and reading is no guarantee you won't come a cropper. But it might help a bit. And it might save us a lot of facebook posts into the bargain.

PART ONE – THE STAGES OF SWIM

Stage one – Fuuuuuck!

There's something utterly elemental about getting into very cold water. The minute it happens, your body will be doing lots of clever things to try to keep you alive, seeing as how you've stupidly apparently just fallen into very cold water. Don't try explaining that it was deliberate, your body won't stop to thank you.

Your brain, when you first start cold water swimming, will be in complete agreement with your body, and will be all in favour of getting out as quickly as possible. You'll likely experience cold water shock, which in extreme cases can cause heart attacks, but in most cases will just make you gasp uncontrollably for a bit. The key thing is to keep your head above water while you gasp. Don't jump into deep cold water, as that way lies drowning. Walk in and stay within your depth as you adjust.

If you're a wild swimmer at heart, you'll have a little shred of curiosity in the back of your mind that will keep you immersed for just a little longer. The same curiosity that got you into this whole wet mess in the first place. It'll be just loud enough to persuade your body… well… why don't we wait and see?

If you persist, particularly through the winter months, your brain will start to disagree with your body when it protests, and become a bit of an insufferable know-it all.

"Dying? You idiot, we're not dying. Don't you remember we did this last week, and we all got out in one piece? We'll not be in long, there's a flask of tea and a hot water bottle wrapped in your pants on the beach, we'll be fine."

Your body won't be interested in shutting up and will persist that it would really rather get out if you don't mind. And, as a human being that lives a pampered life and no longer chases beasts on the plains, has central heating and slippers, and vaccinations, and all the rest of it, it's stupidly invigorating, feeling the pair of them duel it out for survival inside the increasingly chilly skin bag that is you.

Stage two - Peace

They will reach a truce, eventually, your mind and body, if you practice long enough.

You'll be able to rest in a strange moment where you know your body is very cold, but it's not uncomfortable. What's actually happening, is that your blood is all pooling in your core and keeping your organs warm so you don't feel like you're super-cold (yup, clever, told you, we'll come back to this later). You're not shivering, but you're still very much aware that you're in the winter sea.

Anyone who's been for a run on a cold day knows the feeling – when you strip off the layers, your skin is cold to the touch, but you're huffing like a beast and roasting from the inside out.

For anyone like me, who struggles with winter, it's a small victory, committed with your own flesh, against the dying of the sun. A moment you actually stop, suspended in time and water, and notice that your incredible body contains a source of heat and life and survival.

This is all very well, but you can only keep it up for so long.

Stage three - You're *not* turning back into a sea mammal, you're borderline hypothermic

Unfortunately, like most know-it-alls, your mind will get what's coming to it, and quickly. If you ignore your body's pleas for too long, your water-loving mind will lose all reason and start to kill you. You'll start to feel absolutely fucking incredible. Like you could swim forever. Like you're probably kind of super-human actually, and this is really just so lovely and you'll probably just stay in for a few minutes longer and make the most of it even though everyone else has already got out, and…

and…

and…

There will come a gutting moment, all being well, when a sensible inner voice cuts in and breaks it to you that you're not, in fact, immortal, or a dolphin, and you're really very cold even if you don't think so, and would you please get out right now, before you become very mortal indeed?

And if you don't? Hello hypothermia. If you're feeling unusually glad to be alive all of a sudden – and not necessarily giddy with euphoria, maybe just extremely happy with yourself and world – you're already on your way. If you don't get out right now, both the feeling of gladness and quite possibly the feeling of being alive could be short-lived.

Stage four - The art of getting out

There is no greater skill in life than knowing when to leave, and that's certainly the case when swimming.

Trying to explain to new wild swimmers when best to get out of cold water is like trying to read a poem backwards in a mirror with the lights half out, in another language. And your top's just slipped and your boob's hanging out and your chin is inexplicably covered in sand (No, that last one's doing a handstand at sea, sorry).

Getting out is a procedure that can only ever be reverse-engineered. You'll only get feedback if you get it wrong, and you might be dead by then, so it's of limited use. You can only know how to get it right through practice, and even then you have to learn it despite the general lack of useful signs from your mind, body, or indeed the jellyfish (though Lord knows we've tried to train them in this but they're just not on board). After all, if you felt you cold when you got in, how do you know when you're cold enough to warrant getting out?

Basically, if you think you got out too soon, you got it right.

More usefully, since this is supposed to be a book of advice: The best way to work it out is to start small, with just a quick dook. Go in, get past the 'fuuuuuck' stage, if you can, splash around momentarily, then get out. Observe how you feel as you warm up.

Feeling strangely vacant? Still cold hours later? Generally a bit wobbly and not quite right? Feet gone yellow? Lips gone blue? Navel gone green? (I made the last one up, but not the rest). These are all signs you stayed in too long and got too cold. Get out sooner next time.

If none of the above, and you're left with a nagging feeling that you 'had a bit more in you' and could've stayed in longer – congratulations, you got it exactly right!

My view, and that of most experienced wild swimmers, is that it's a bad idea to start in winter. Cold water can be lethal and your only defence is experience. Hypothermia can arrive swiftly, and without warning, and one of its key symptoms is confusion, which will render you unable to summon help. Start in summer and carry on regularly as the water gets colder so that you can acclimatise and learn what your body feels like in cold water.

Be aware that sea temperatures tend to lag a little behind seasonal air temperatures – it's proper cold in there at least through the end of March, and into April. It warms slowly, becoming a little more amenable to hardy beginners around May, and peaking from July to September.

As you move from summer into winter, you have to kind of back up into this whole thing, cutting your time in the water drastically as temperatures drop.

It's a matter of debate, I think, how you achieve this magical thing called Getting Out In Time. Some people like the security of swimming with a watch. After all, how do you know how to get out sooner if you're not timing it?

But I don't wear a watch, because I think the variables of water temperature, air temperature, wind chill, menstrual cycle, what you've eaten, how you've slept, if you're hungover, and a million other things, can make your tolerance vary so much, that measuring minutes from one week to the next is as good as useless.

For a similar reason, many experienced swimmers are unimpressed by the rule you'll sometimes hear touted of swimming for "one minute per degree of water temperature". It can do more harm than good if it stops you paying attention to your own swim as it unfolds, because you're assuming that your watch will tell you when you're cold.

I have an internal clock ticking away inside me that pretty much does the job instead. For me, it ticks through roughly the following phases, not unlike this book:

Fuuuuuck!
Internal debate on what I think I'm up to, coming face to
face with my own soul
Getting over it, achieving momentary peace
Bobbing over here
Bobbing over there
Doing a handstand
Thinking I feel fine, it's a shame to get out now, therefore
I shall get out.

And that stands me in pretty good stead. It just so
happens that, in winter, once the water dips below about
10C, I reckon all of that probably takes about five minutes.
But I'm not sure, because I've not timed it. In summer, the
bobbing and the handstands stretch out longer – the whole
thing might be 30 minutes? I've no idea. I just know when
it happens, and how I feel when I'm done – both in terms
of how much fun I've had, and what sensations my body is
experiencing.

Your own internal clock will vary, and the only way to
find out what it has to say to you, is to get started, in a
such a way that you don't get hypothermia while you do it.

Observe how your body feels during the swim, how you
feel at the point you get out, and compare those with your
recovery. Rinse and repeat. Start small, pay attention, build
up gradually, swim with others. Take care of yourself, and
them.

It's worth noting that our capacity to stay in cold water
for any length of time is always changing. Some
experienced wild swimmers feel they acclimatise year on
year, getting better able to withstand the cold the more
winters they swim through.

However, some researchers think that what's actually
happening is that they don't get better at conserving their
body temperature – they just get better at staying physically
comfortable while their temperature drops. This can be a
useful adaptation in some ways – if your mind is clear and

your hands still agile, it's easier to get dressed and warm again. But it also raises the possibility of you feeling just dandy while your temperature is dangerously low.

In that case, counter-intuitively, more experienced swimmers could be at greater risk from hypothermia than new swimmers, who left the water shivering convulsively five minutes earlier.

The fact researchers are still unpicking this only goes to show that none of us can be complacent. You must stay alert, get to know what works for *you*, and – most importantly – get out before you feel you need to.

Stage five - The afterdrop

They speak of it late at night, the gnarly old swimmers, gathered around their bonfires, yellowed fingers clasped around flasks of hot Ribena, rocking from foot to foot like a flock of dry robe-smothered penguins. Lapsing into bad West Country accents, like folk out the pub on An American Werewolf in London, they'll ask "'Ave you 'eard.... of the afterdrop?" and a hushed gasp will sweep across the beach.

Nah, I made that up. It's not a monster. But you should respect it. And know about it. And prepare for it. It's got a cool name, after all, what's not to love?

So. Let's learn a little bit about what happens to your body when you get into cold water. I mentioned somewhere upstream about all the clever things your body does when you get into cold water. Right up there on the list, is vasoconstriction. About the time your body is getting into a yelling match with your mind about whether to stay in the water, your blood vessels will narrow, allowing less blood through to your extremities.

This makes sure plenty of nice warm blood stays in your torso, keeping your all-important vital organs warm (Clue's in the name: Vital. Nobody wants to live without their fingertips, but it's probably preferable to life without your liver or lungs. Your body's a natural prioritiser).

So your organs are warm and surrounded by blood, your extremities cool and vasoconstricted. That's why, once you hit that moment of peace, you feel kind of cold-but-not-cold all at once. Your organs, just for that moment, are doing OK, kept warm by more than their fair share of your blood supply. It won't last forever, but you're warm inside for a moment, even as your arms and legs are aware of the cold.

Then you get out. Your body knows it, and the vasoconstriction releases. It's party time for your blood vessels! Imagine your local, the day after the end of lockdown – all those folk who haven't seen each other for ages just can't wait to get a-mingling with each other again. And so it is with your circulation – it gets… well, circulating. All that warm blood from your core is allowed to move around again. Which means all that cold blood from your extremities is moving too. And sooner or later, it's going to hit your core.

Holy crap, it's cold. Bone deep, gut chilling, struggle-to-keep-the-heid cold.

This is the afterdrop.

It usually hits at around the time you're standing on the beach with your cossie around your ankles, your robe round your neck with one arm out, the wind whipping your hair in your eyes, your clothes - which you left perfectly laid out – mysteriously now tangled in a damp, twisted, pile of sand in your Ikea bag, and all sense rapidly draining from your mind.

The afterdrop isn't necessarily a sign you've been in too long – it's an inevitable part of cold water swimming, and you have to prepare for it by getting out while you've still got some body temperature to spare, rather than waiting until you feel uncomfortably cold.

Your core temperature will drop measurably after you get out of the water, and the shivering may start. (That's no bad thing, by the way – shivering generates warmth in your muscles. Complete absence of shivering when you're intensely cold can be more of a worry.)

You will have an urge to huddle into yourself and stand there, frozen, waiting until you feel a bit warmer to get dressed. Don't. You need to get yourself warm.

Stage six - Warming up

The afterdrop, numb fingers and the apparent ability of your clothes to all move around in your bag on their own while you were out swimming, are all reasons that, when it comes to warming up, you need a plan. When I get out, the first things I do, in order, are:

* Stick on a towelling robe
* Strip off my wet cossie beneath it
* Take my swim hat off, put a woolly hat on
* Take a good swig of a hot drink

After that, I'm more relaxed. Next priority is to get your core – your torso – warm and dry. So dry your chest and tummy and back, and dress your top half in everything you have before you do anything else. Yes, this means you'll find yourself standing on the beach in a puffa jacket and underpants. If you expected to get through this with your dignity intact, you're in the wrong place, my friend. Wrong. Place.

Side note: Actually, who ever put on underpants after a wild swim? Or a bra? Nobody. File under mistakes you'll never make twice. But thanks anyway to the complete stranger who helped me that time I was trapped in my sports bra at Threipmuir reservoir.

You should always have way more warm clothes than you think you'll need. Gloves and a woolly hat are often useful even in summer. Thermals, warm socks, big boots, winter coats. Wool is good because it keeps you warm even when wet. Bring as much as you can. Keep swigging that hot drink as you go.

I think I am probably, at this stage, alone among the wild swimming community in not owning a dry robe. I am thus never able to participate in the regular and unwitting re-enactments of the summer solstice at Stonehenge as everyone troops off the beach in their matching hooded cloaks, but there we go. I understand they're magical and will warm you up a treat. Price and bulk are the downsides, but maybe one day I'll succumb. They certainly seem a good option for warming up with minimal faff.

It's always tempting, once you get home, to dive straight for a hot shower or bath to warm up. Do not be tempted. It'll make your skin feel warm, but it'll have very little effect on your core. In fact, the very opposite of vasoconstriction will kick in. All those peripheral blood vessels will open up and your blood will flood outwards, away from your still-chilly core, leaving you feeling noticeably unwarmed by the whole escapade. This change in blood flow can also cause a drop in blood pressure and make you feel faint.

I don't want to go full on 'The things I've seeeeen....." at this point, but I'm going to anyway, because among the things I've seen are one friend's face turning an extraordinary shade of grey as we huddled under the hot swimming pool showers in The Early Days, after getting out of the sea. We knew no better. Also another friend's hand unnervingly appearing under the bottom of her changing cubicle when she was supposed to be getting dressed. She'd warmed up too fast and realised the only way she was going to stay not-fainted was to cease being upright and sit down on the floor for a bit.

So – warm up gradually. Eat and drink warm things, put on plenty of layers, maybe nudge the heat up a wee bit. But stay away from the hot water.

Stage seven – The shivery bite

The shivery bite is the glorious finale of any swimming experience: A post-swim snack, clutched in icy fingers, eased between chattering teeth and mumbling blue lips.

A cake or biscuit – or even a sandwich for the savoury among us – that revives and uplifts. Packed especially for this glorious moment when we give an exploratory wiggle of our toes, stand and look back at the water, and think: "I was just in there! *Me!* In *there!*"

And the sugar hits our stomachs and our body rejoices and our soul soars and they are, in the presence of our sacramental shivery bite, united and whole once more.

PART TWO – MISCELLANEOUS

We are not a club

For such a clubbable group of people, we are very much opposed to anyone who even so much as looks at us, in a way that suggests we might be a club.

I can only speak for the groups I help admin, but I'm pretty sure we're not alone. There are many facebook groups set up all over the country to help wild swimmers find one another and share advice, but they are just that – a loose collection of individuals who like doing the same thing. No insurance, no coaching, no responsibility for telling you how not to hurt yourself while at your new hobby (though we will, of course, do what we can to help you on that score). I've lost count of the number of times I've typed the phrases 'You are responsible for your own safety' and 'Make your own call'. Usually IN CAPS, I'm not ashamed to admit.

It's not just because we're enthusiastic amateurs who don't get paid for this shit (though it is definitely because of that). It's also because we don't know. Water is wild and unpredictable, and none of us are oceanographers or meteorologists (except for the oceanographers and meteorologists, but they're swimming off the clock). Just because we haven't posted a warning of a developing rip tide or a touring pod of orcas today, doesn't mean they're not there. So. We are not a club. MAKE YOUR OWN CALL.

Jellyfish

Let's be honest, they were here first (Note to self: Were they? Must read up about evolution – when did we actually leave the sea?)

Anyway, at the end of the day, we're in their world, and we owe them some respect. They don't have the option to slop out of the sea and drag themselves up to McDonald's for a day out, so if we will insist on intruding on their manor, let's not moan about finding them out for a swim when we get there.

Everyone who's swum in the sea for a bit has their own tale of their first ever jellyfish kiss. (Me: Back of the hands, Portobello, Edinburgh. Wasn't sure at first I'd been stung as my hands were so cold I couldn't really feel them. But then I saw some pink tendrils on my wetsuit and knew I'd been inducted into the way of the jellyfish. I know – wetsuit but no gloves, not the other way around, what was I thinking? What can I say, it was The Early Days).

There's NHS advice online about what to do if you're stung by jellyfish or other sea crittas. It might get updated, in the way medical advice sometimes does, so you're probably better off looking it up afresh, but right now, they suggest: Rinsing it with sea water (not fresh water); scraping any spines off with tweezers or the edge of a bank card; soaking the area in very warm water – as hot as you can stand - for at least 30 minutes (use wet towels if you're not able to soak), and taking paracetamol or ibuprofen. Be aware that people's reactions to jellyfish stings may vary and some people can be allergic and suffer more serious consequences, so keep an eye on yourself and each other after a sting.

The weird ways the water moves

Now, I'll come clean here and admit that I'm not an expert on rip tides, regular tides, currents, or anything of the sort. Which is certainly a disadvantage when writing a book about staying safe at sea. However, I do have some very good advice for you:

Seek advice.

Even if I knew everything about the sea, I wouldn't know anything about *your* sea (or all the other places you love to swim). Every beach is different. Every river or loch is different. Every season is different. Hell, every day is different. So ask around. Ask surfers – they're brilliant, they've been watching the waves for years, they know when a swell is coming, which way the wind will be blowing, what the tides are up to, and what that'll mean for conditions on and off shore.

Ask local people, swimmers and non-swimmers, what they know about the water and how it behaves. Ask your local sailing club, or coastal rowers, or coastguard, or fisherfolk, or anyone who has knowledge of local conditions.

Make observations of your own, both in and out of the water. Before you swim, look up tide tables, notice the wind speed and direction in the weather forecast, Google your nearest surf forecast and find out how high the swell is. When you're in, notice how it feels, how big and how strong the waves are, which way the current's pulling, what the surface of the water looks like. Get to know your water, but remember it can – and will – still surprise you.

Assess constantly. Don't be afraid to change your mind at the last minute or even during your swim. The water will always be there tomorrow.

A few other (very much non-exhaustive) things gleaned over the years:

Tides: If you swim out perpendicular to the shore, it might feel easy getting to your destination, but when you turn around, if the tide's going out, it'll be much harder getting back in again. Easy to forget, until you're out of your depth and swimming on the spot like you're on some kind of aquatic treadmill.

Rip tides: Weird beasts, a current in a particular part of the beach that'll pull you away from the shore. They're often marked by a calm patch of water with waves either side, but really don't just listen to my advice on this one, look them up online, there's loads of good information including videos and diagrams and all sorts. The most important thing to remember if you get caught in one is – don't try to swim straight towards the shore – you'll lose that battle. Swim sideways, parallel to the shore, and you should exit the rip. If that's too tough, lie on your back so you float, and wait until you feel the rip easing up. Then swim out to the side.

Reservoirs: Can have submerged equipment that you could injure yourself on, and the water level can fluctuate wildly, so something that was safely out of reach of your dangling legs or diving face one day might be closer to the surface another day. Reservoirs will also have some kind of outflow. You don't want to be anywhere near this if it is suddenly opened up and water's being drained out of the reservoir at a rapid rate – you'll be in danger of getting dragged down.

Water quality

Well, quite frankly, who knows half the time? Some beaches are certified clean and spangly, others never get so much as a test from one year to the next.

Plenty of places seem to fall off the bottom of the cleanliness charts but hardy swimmers will tell you they've never got ill from swimming there (Oh, except that one time, but it was only a week off work, and hey, maybe it was the mussels they ate the day before, they're not really sure, and the paralysis has almost gone now anyway).

Obviously, if water quality is measured in your area, you're ahead of the game. You do just need be sure what you're looking at when you read the measurement. It might be a very general description of the water quality at a given beach, based on samples taken over a long period (and so not a description of specifically how the water is today compared to yesterday). It might be a precise measurement of water quality samples on previous specific dates. Or it might be a prediction of today's likely water quality based on recent weather, and/or euphemistically-titled 'pollution events' eg. a breakdown at the local sewage plant.

Some things that we do know:

Water quality is generally markedly worse for a couple of days after heavy rain because it washes crap (both literally and figuratively) off the fields, into the rivers, and into the sea.

There are places (shout-out to Edinburgh!) where, to prevent homes getting flooded with sewage, waste pipes are designed to overflow into storm drains as a last resort in super-heavy rain, and then into the sea. So that's nice.

Clear water doesn't mean clean water (bacteria aren't visible) and murky water doesn't mean dirty water (it could just be stirred-up sand).

You know what this section calls for? I think it's very much a MAKE YOUR OWN CALL situation.

What to wear

From the bather swathed in so much neoprene they can communicate only by blinking, to the one you know wants to skinny dip and is only wearing their Speedos as a concession to not being arrested, wild swimming is a broad church when it comes to attire.

When I first found my wild swim pals around 10 years ago, we assumed a wetsuit was needed for winter, and duly neoprened up for our first year. A decade down the line, most of us have settled on cossie, with neoprene socks and gloves in winter and silicone swim hats.

Did I say wild swimming was going to make you look good? No, I most certainly did not, but frankly, that's one of the great things about it. When you're resigned to walking down the beach effectively wearing your vest, pants, socks, gloves and a jaunty little hat, there's precious little space for worrying about your cellulite or your jelly belly or the fact you accidentally forgot to shave your bikini line for the past 12 years.

That said, fashions change, even in the wild swimming world. There's a recent trend for wearing woolly hats instead of silicone – it's not for me, I like to lie back in the water and stare at the sky – but it's warm and it certainly looks better on Instagram, so each to their own.

The obvious advantage of neoprene is that you get a longer swim, especially in winter. It can seem a hell of a guddle to go all the way to the beach with a big sack of clothes just for the few moments you get in the water in a cossie.

On the other hand, some people want the tang of the salt and the chill of the waves on their skin, and struggling out of a wetsuit can add to the time it takes to get warm and dry. So – find your bliss, wear what you want.

Bobbing and bathing and bombing for the finish

Do you have to be a strong swimmer to swim outdoors? Well find your bliss, do what you want. As long as you stay within your means and don't put yourself or anyone else in danger, anything goes.

I am very much at the bobbing end of things. I get in, I float, I chat. I stay within my depth. I might suddenly get the funny idea that I could get some exercise while I'm swimming and do a few beats of breaststroke. But then I float and chat some more and turn in a couple of handstands before calling it a day and heading back up the sand to find my biscuits.

I've pals who don't enter the water unless they've got a couple of K planned out and a lift at the end to bring them home.

Nobody cares, it's not a competition (obviously in some cases it actually *is* a competition, but in those cases you've probably paid an entry fee and turned up at the start time, so you'll be somewhat aware of the deal). Happily, the wild swim community is generally more united by the love of getting wet than it is divided by judgement of exactly how we all choose to do it. Get wet, have fun, do your thing.

Tidying the beach

Pretty simple, really. Don't leave your rubbish behind and, if you can, take someone else's with you too. Take a bag to the beach, pick up some rubbish and bin it when you can. Even if you swim on a barely-used beach, there'll be a steady stream of stuff washed up by the waves that you can clear away. Maybe if you're one of those arty types you can make a mobile out of it, I don't know.

The final splash

For all the grumblings and warnings contained herein,
wild swimming has changed my life, and the lives of so
many people I know, immeasurably for the better.

It is joy, it is friendship, it is loving your body and the sky
and the birds and the seals and that thermal top you
bought 20 years ago that's still going strong.

For me and my friends, it's been weddings and funerals.
It's been sickness and health and bonfires and tears and
being alone and being together – and at the end of the day,
what is more important than all of that?

Stay safe, because your swimming friends need you.

Printed in Great Britain
by Amazon

18426921R10020